I0502696

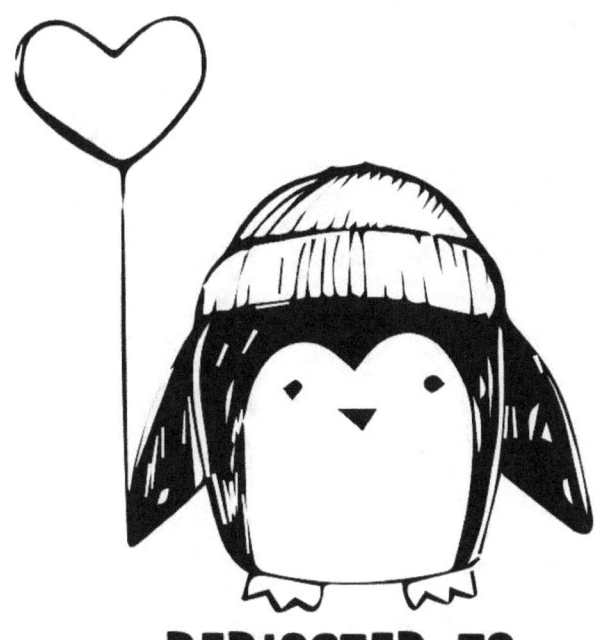

DEDICATED TO
SASHA AND ELLA'S

IF YOU LOVE THIS BOOK

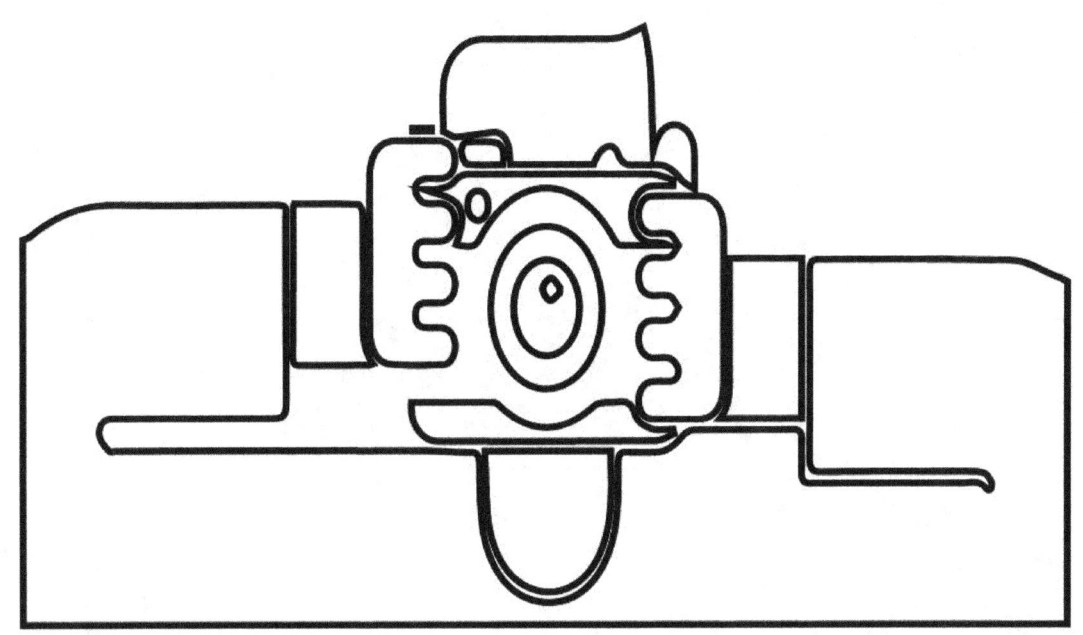

PLEASE TAKE A PICTURE AND SHARE
YOUR FINISHED ART WITH US ON AMAZON
WE WANT TO HEAR WHAT YOU LOVE
ABOUT OUR COLORING BOOKS!

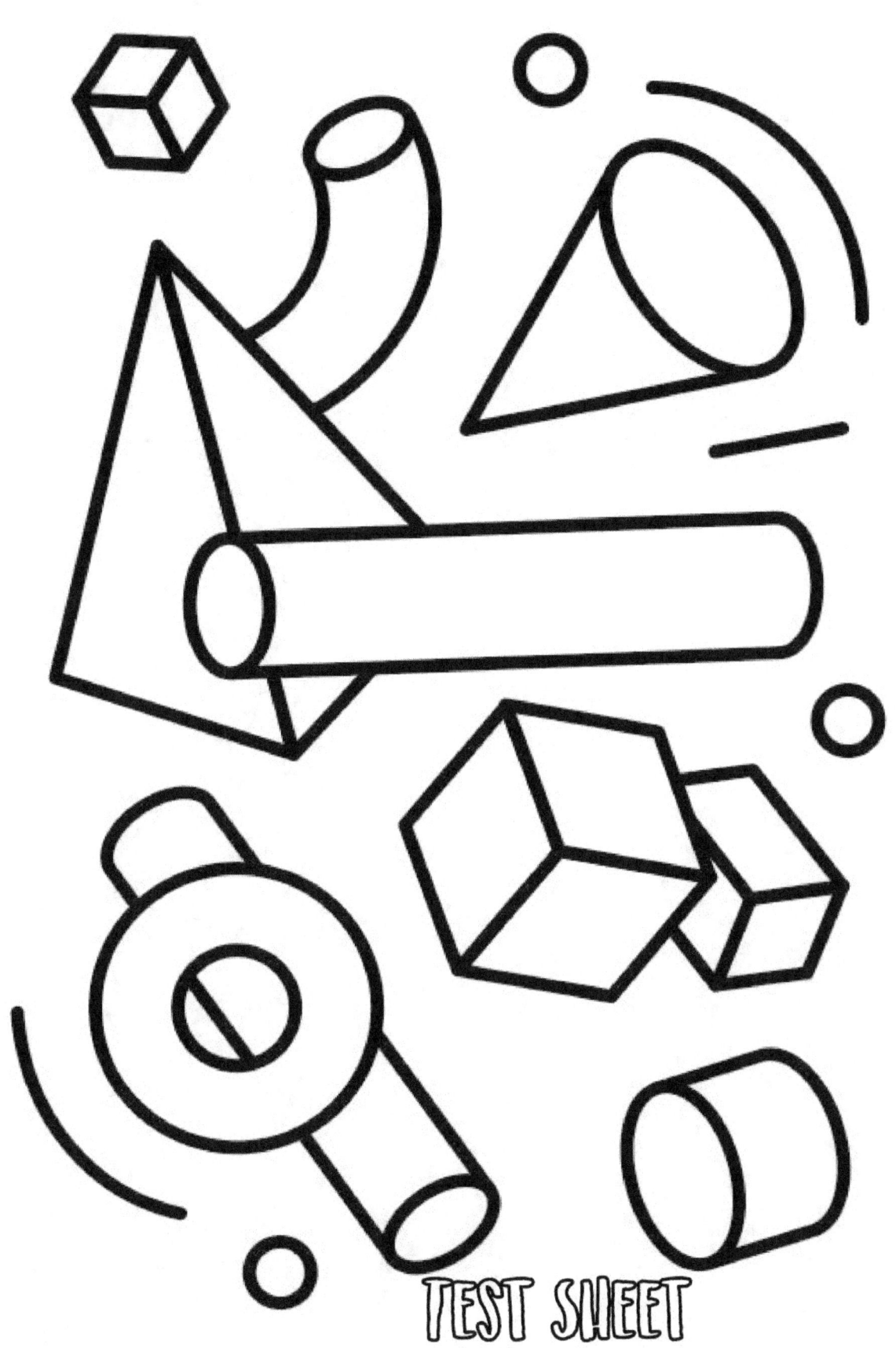

TEST SHEET

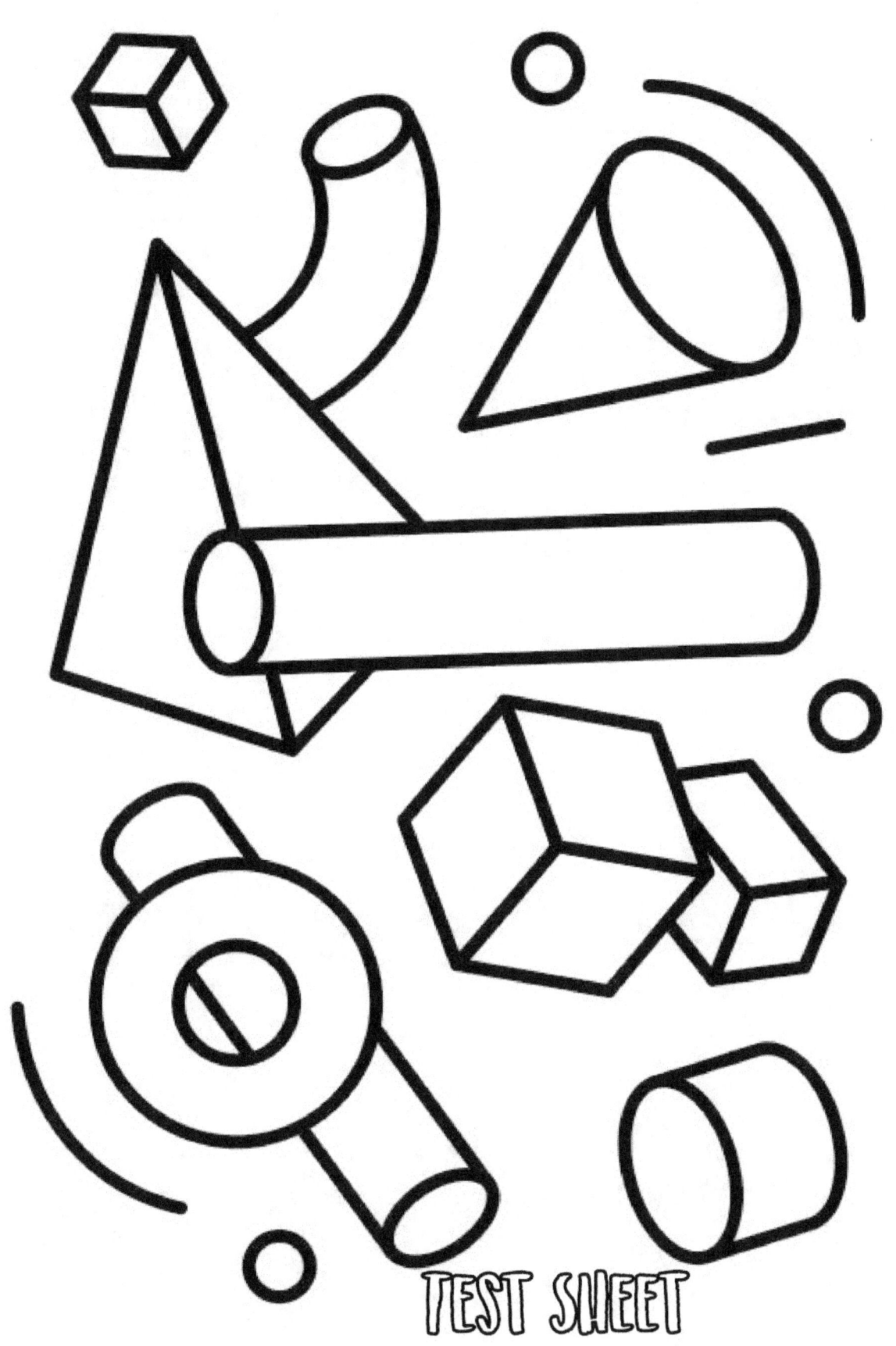

TEST SHEET

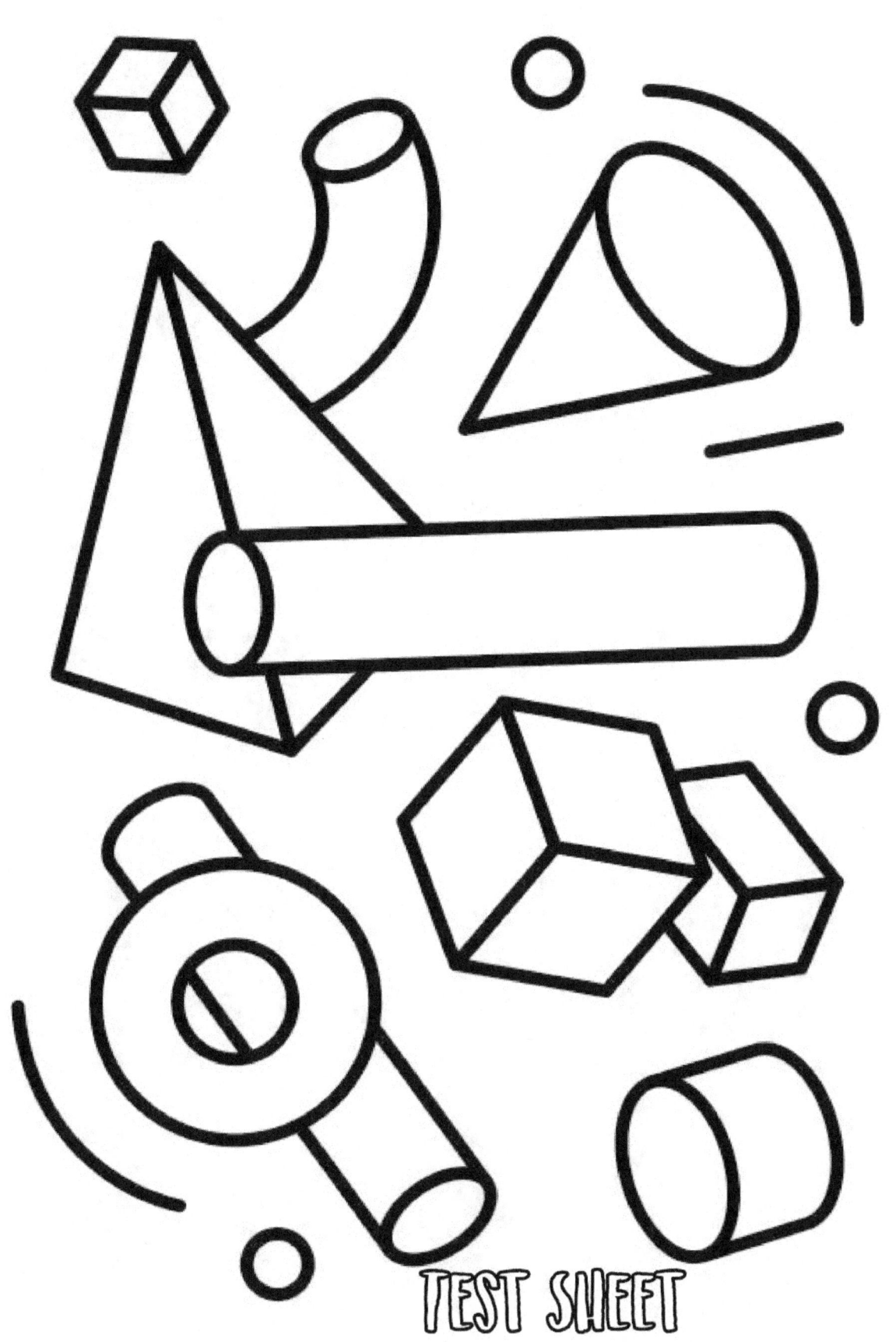

TEST SHEET

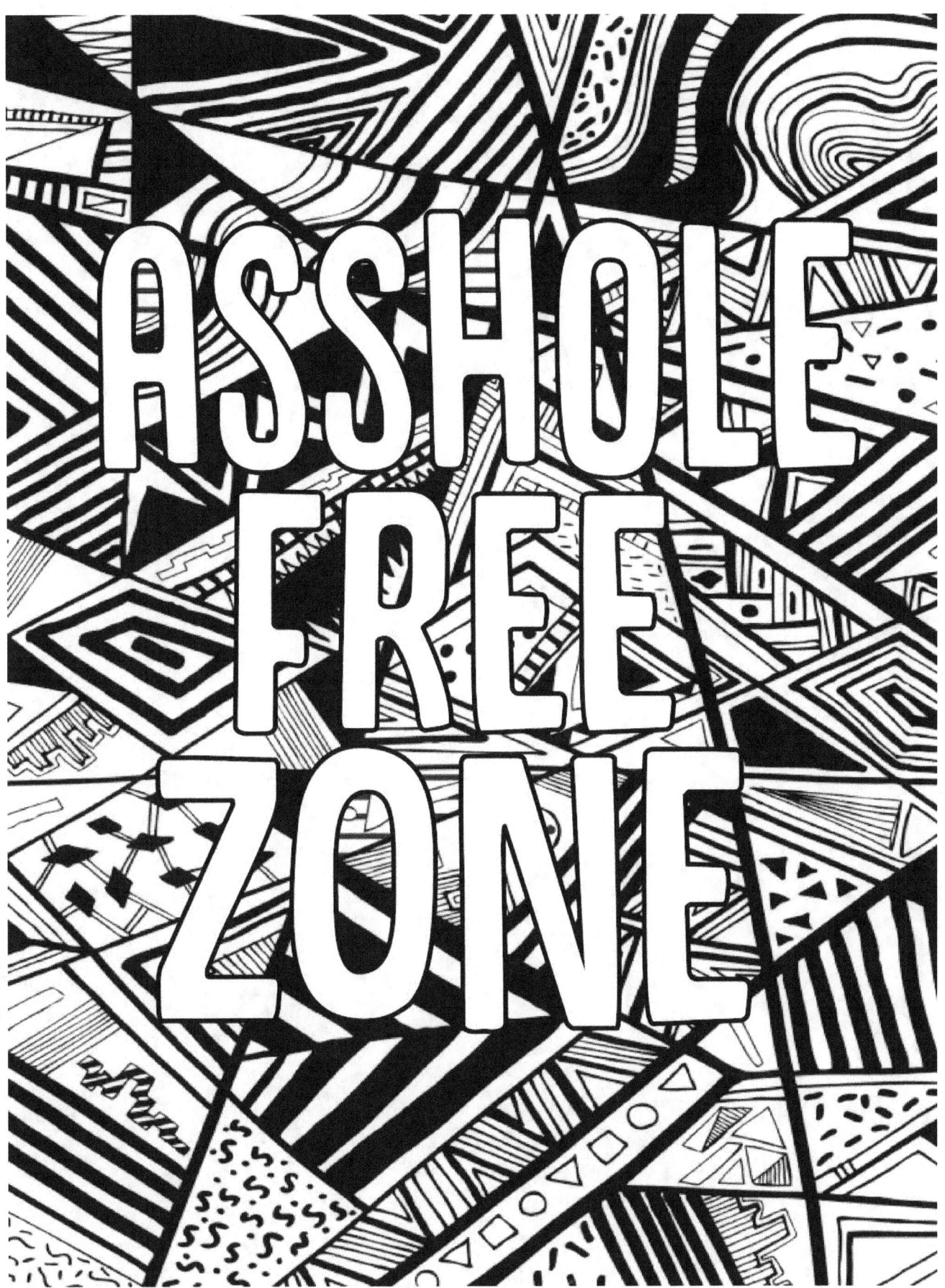

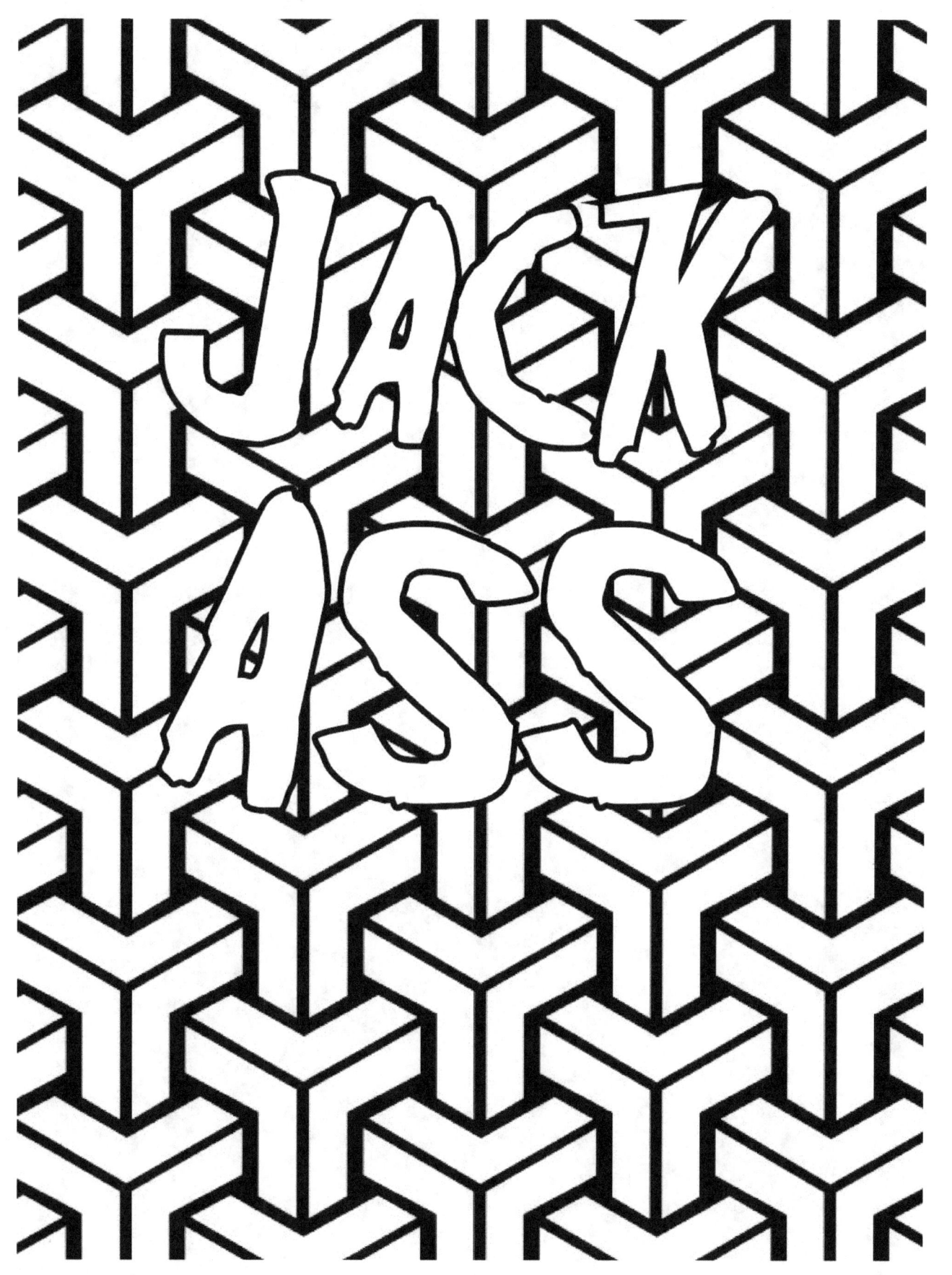

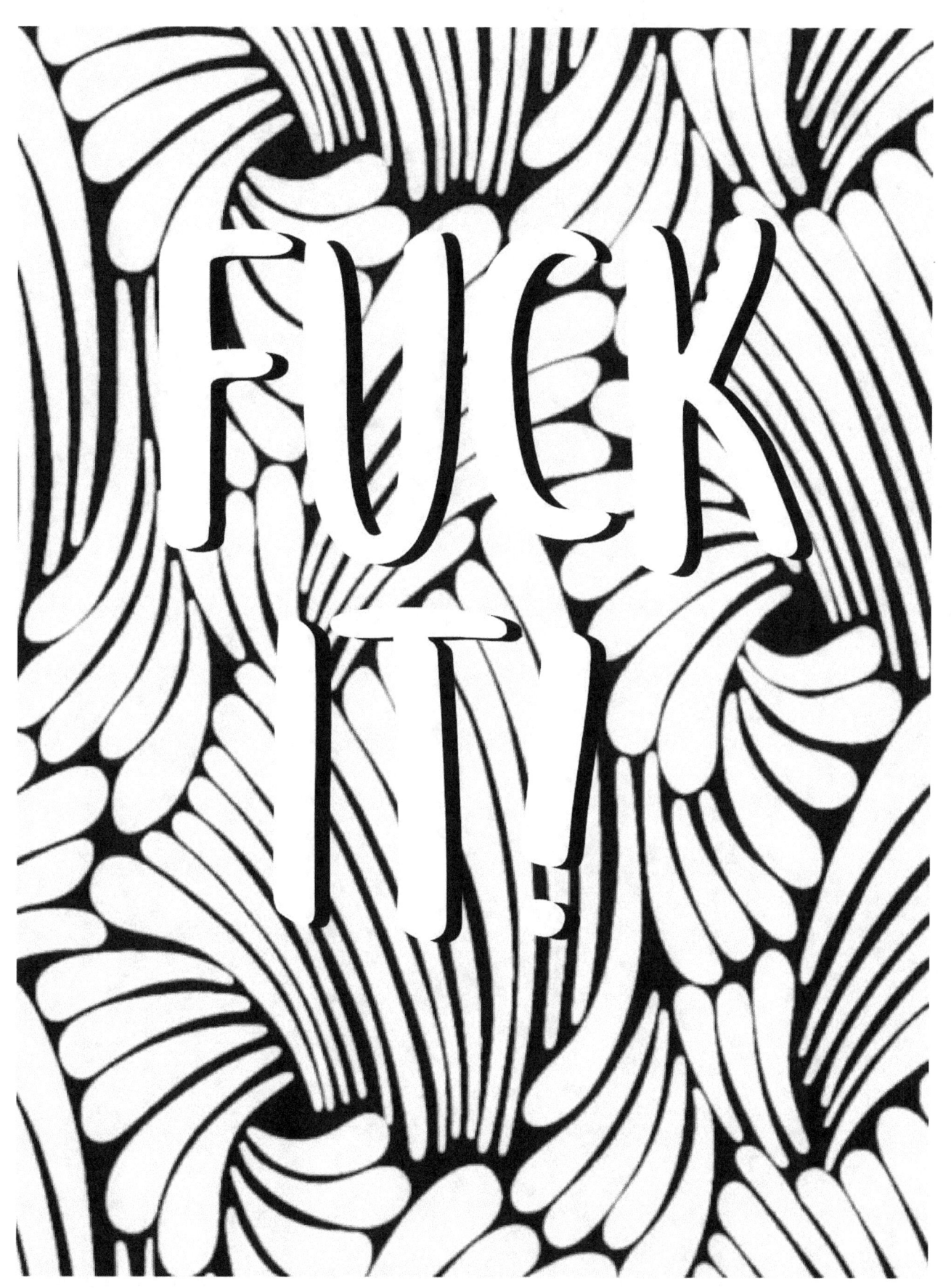

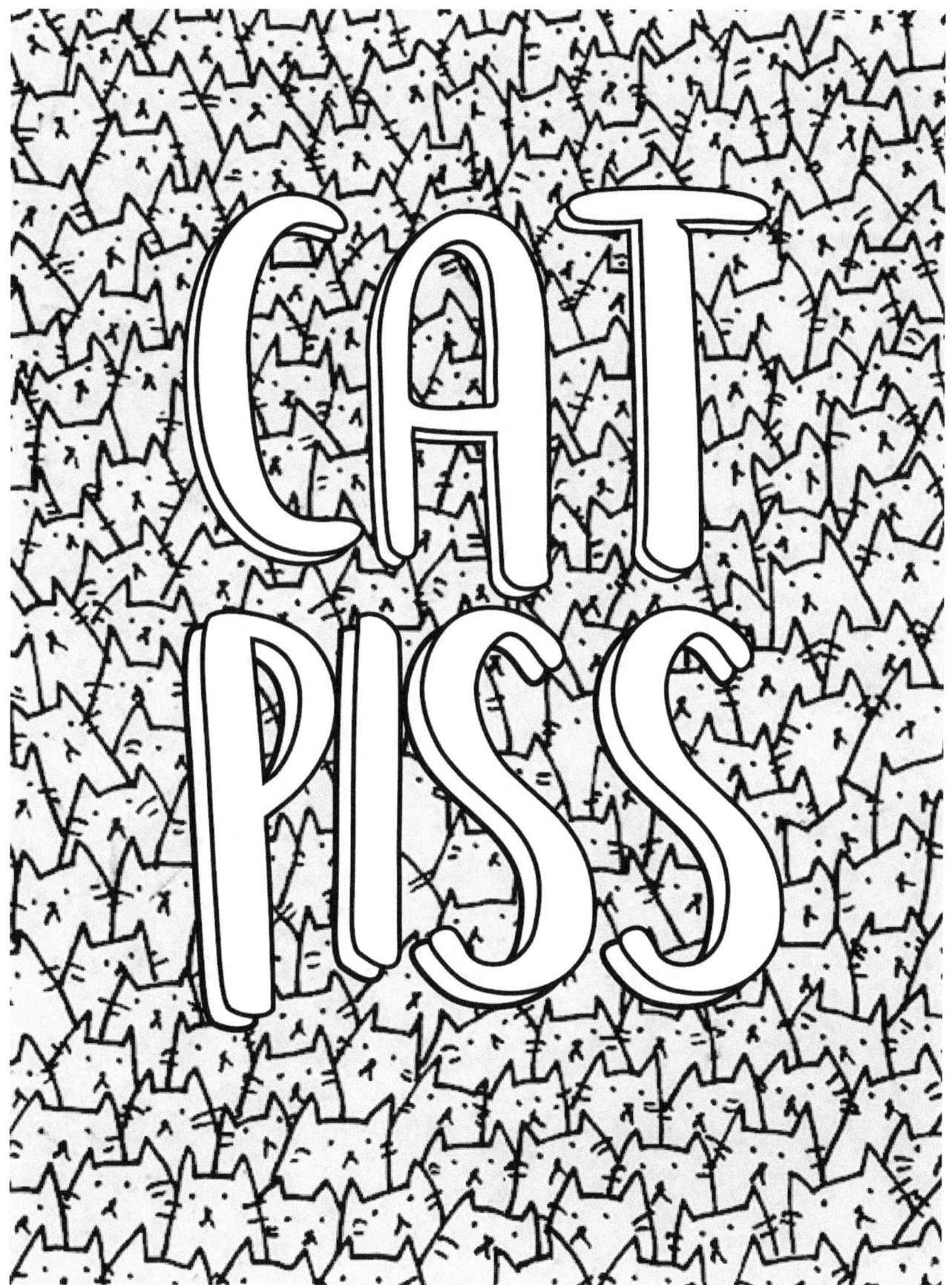

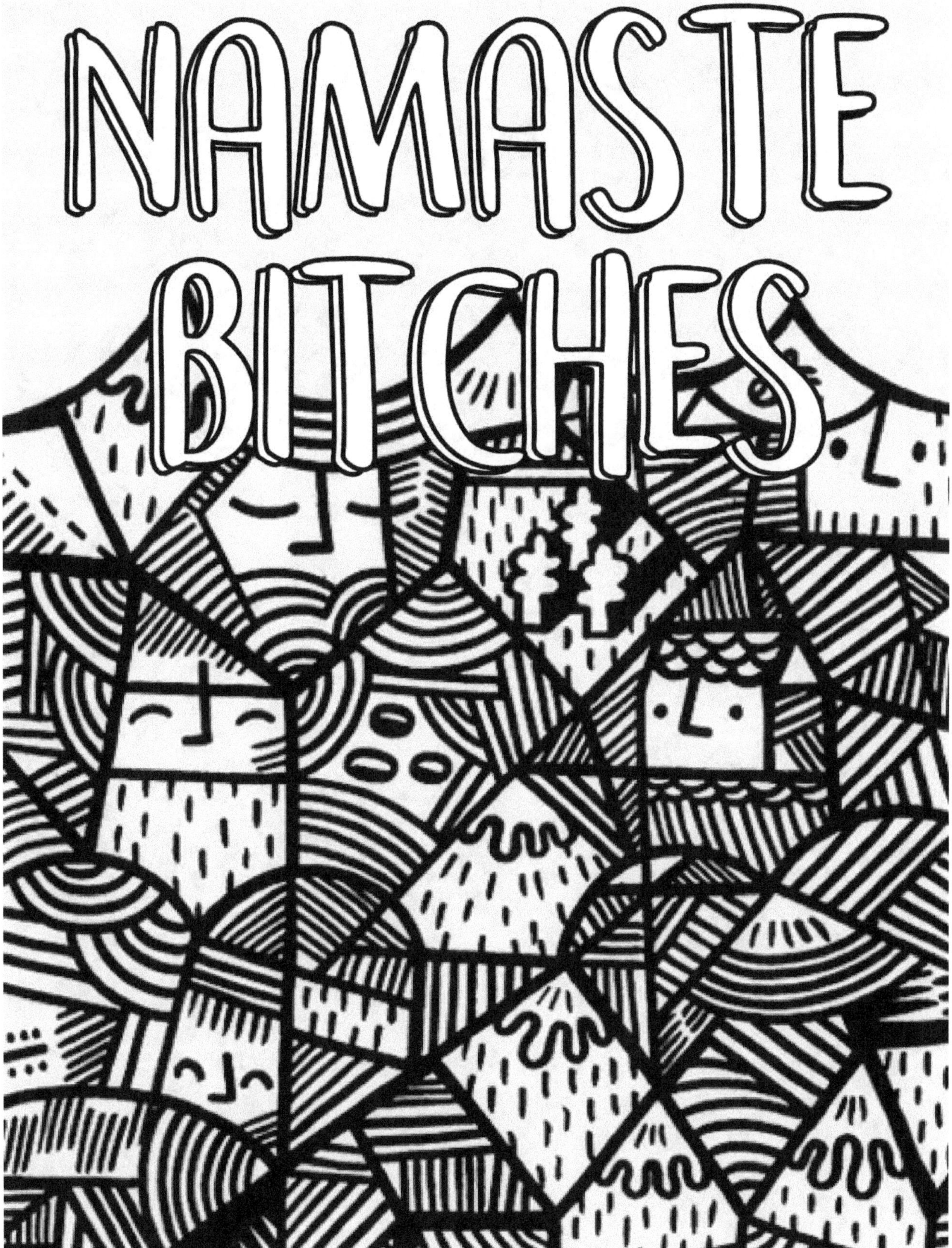
NAMASTE
BITCHES

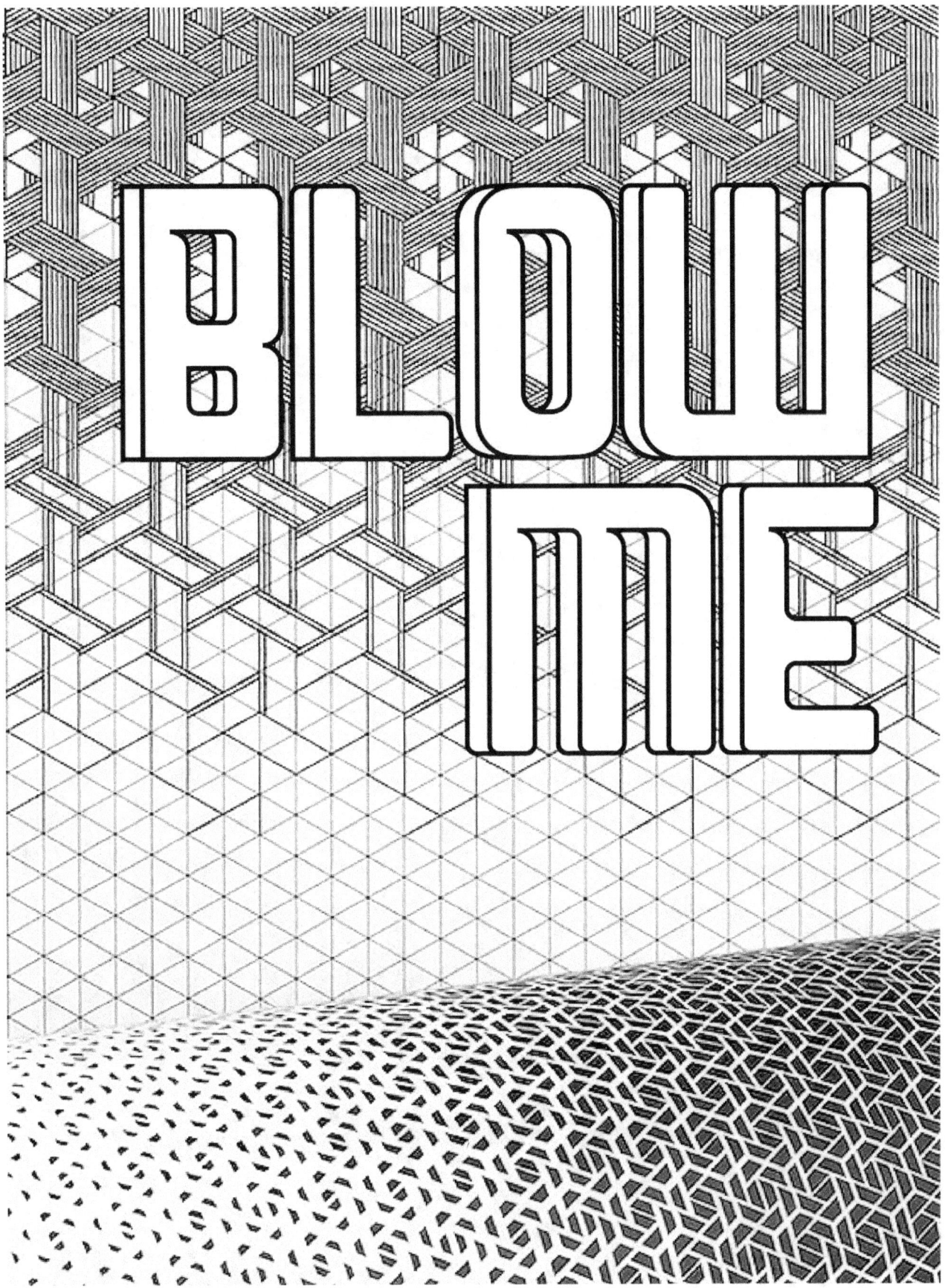

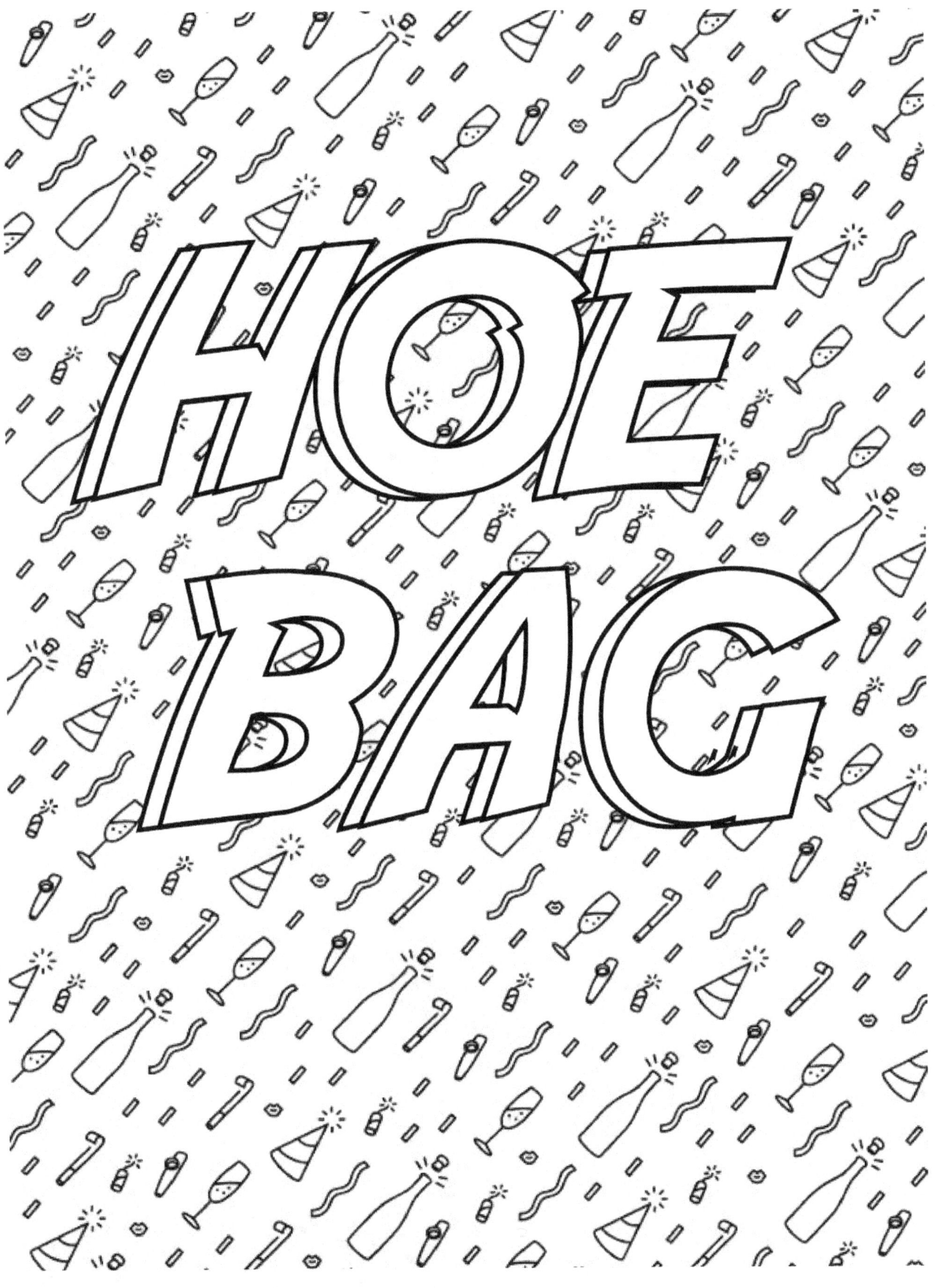

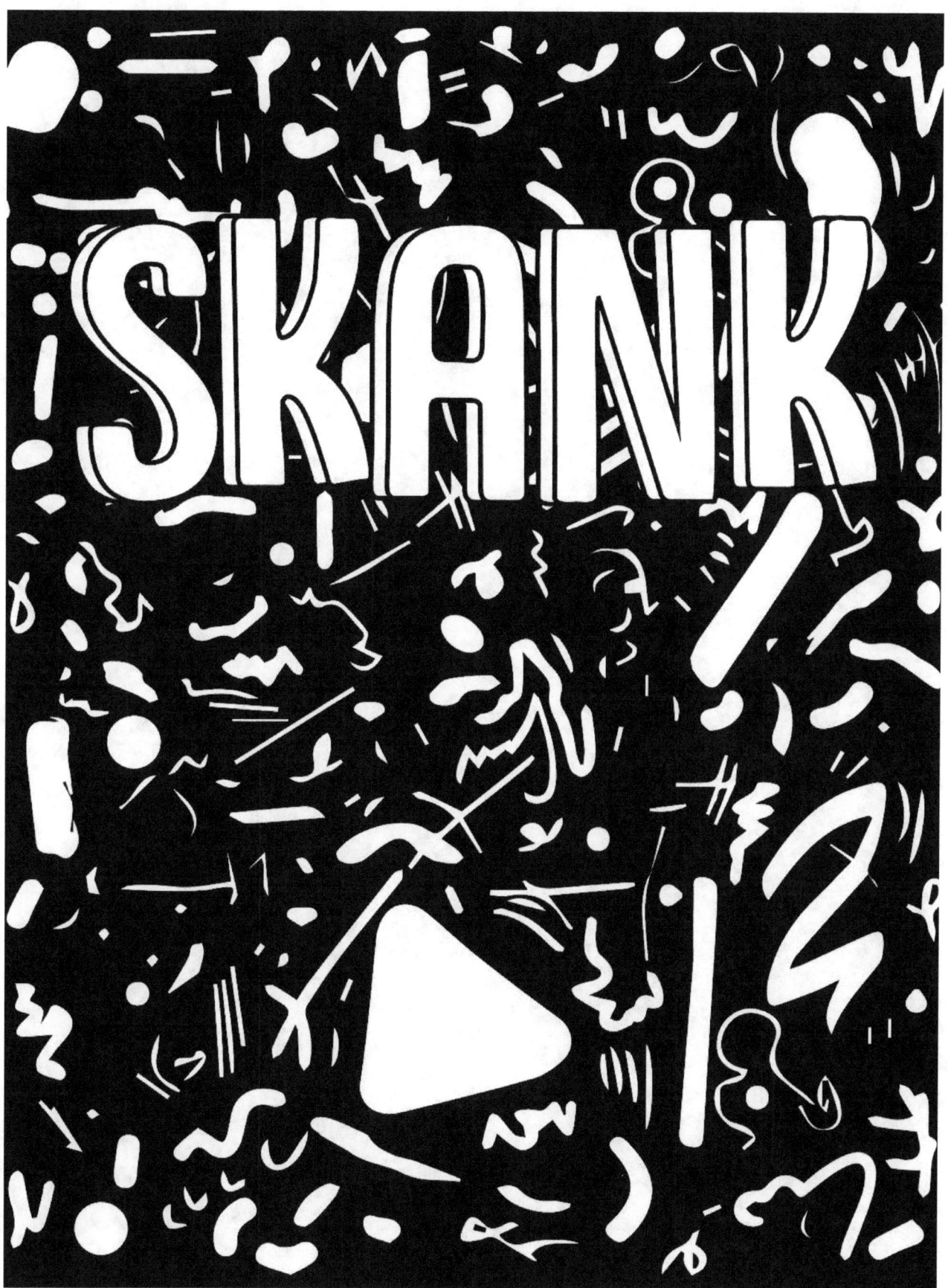

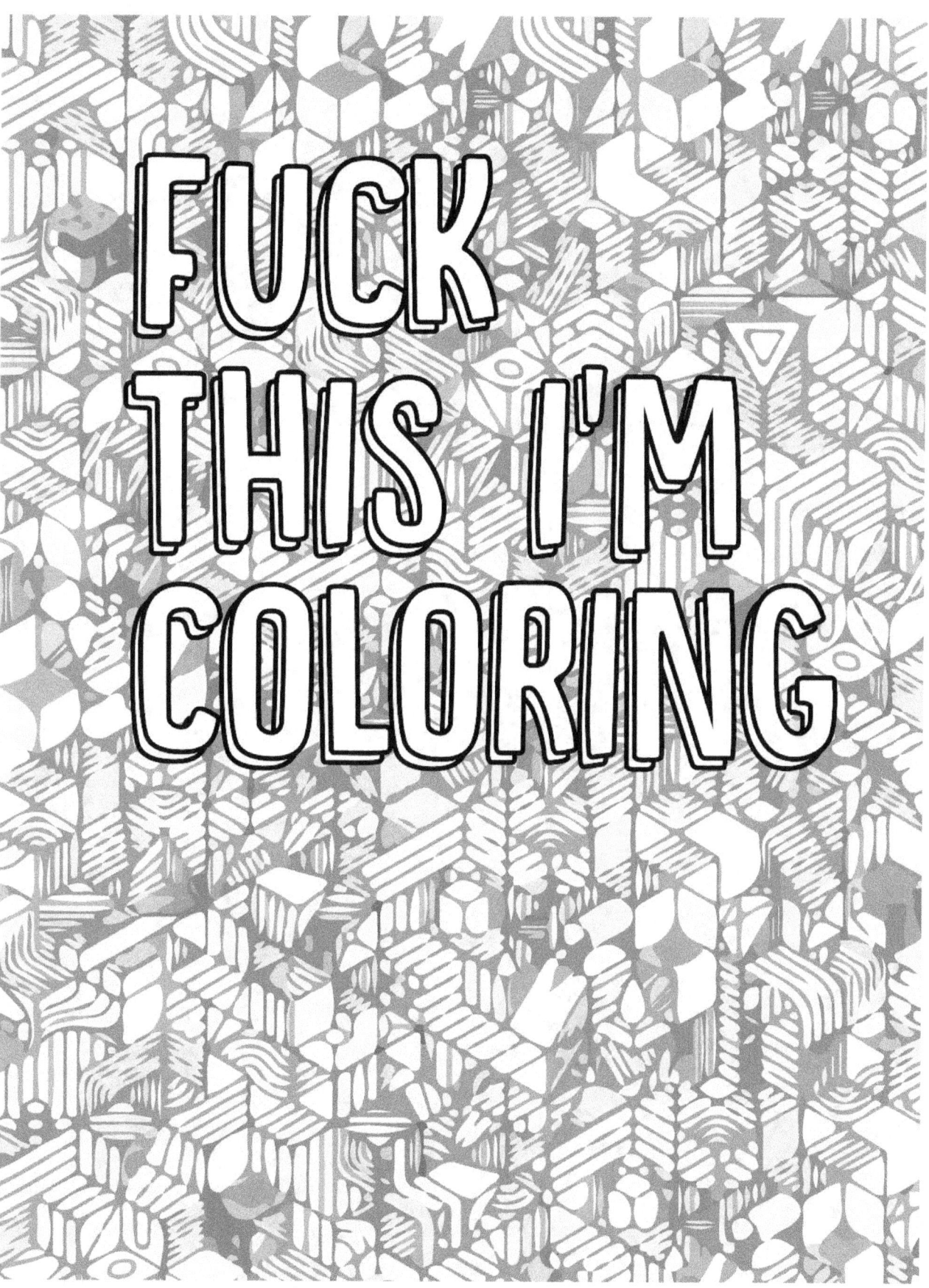

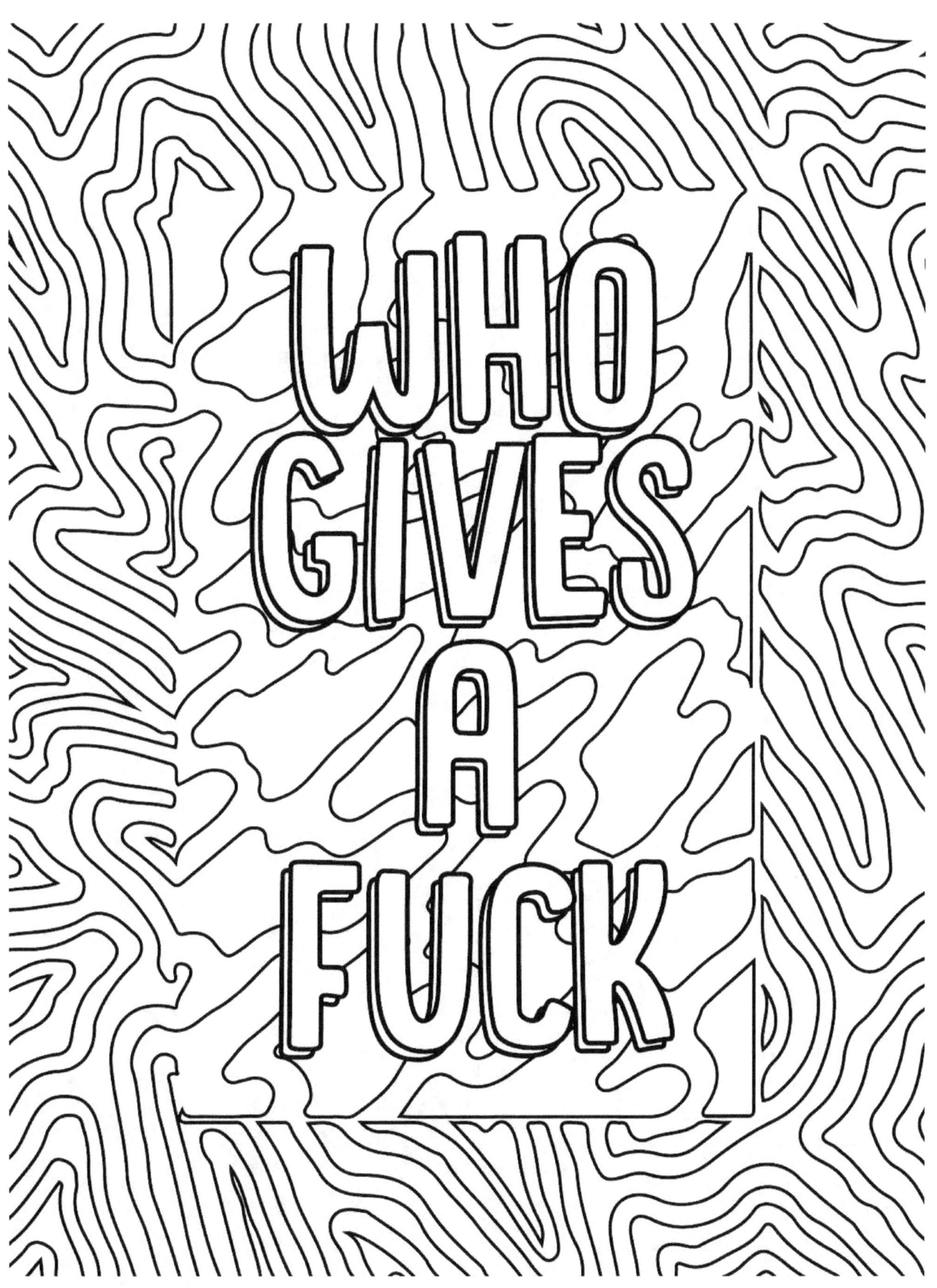

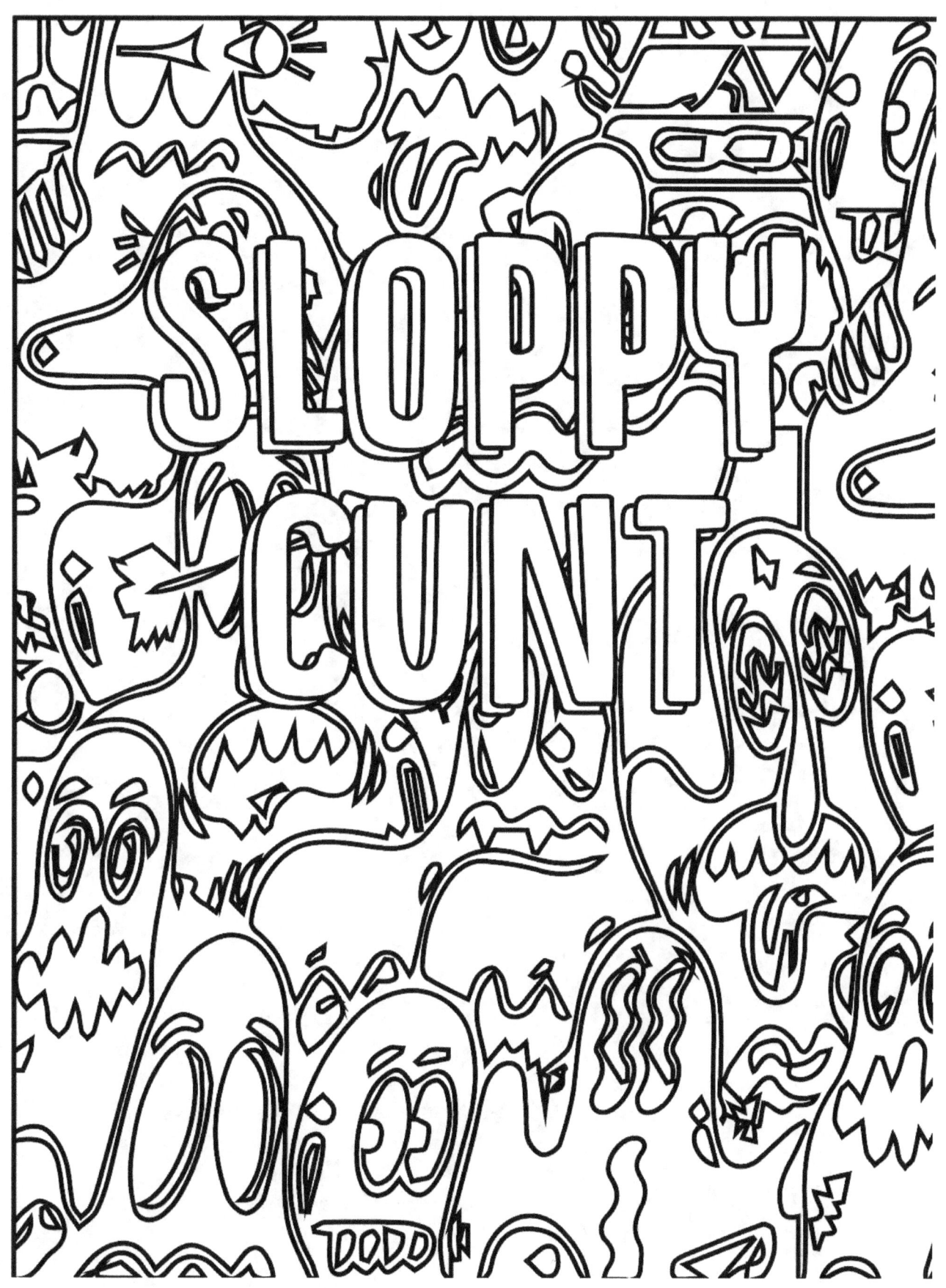

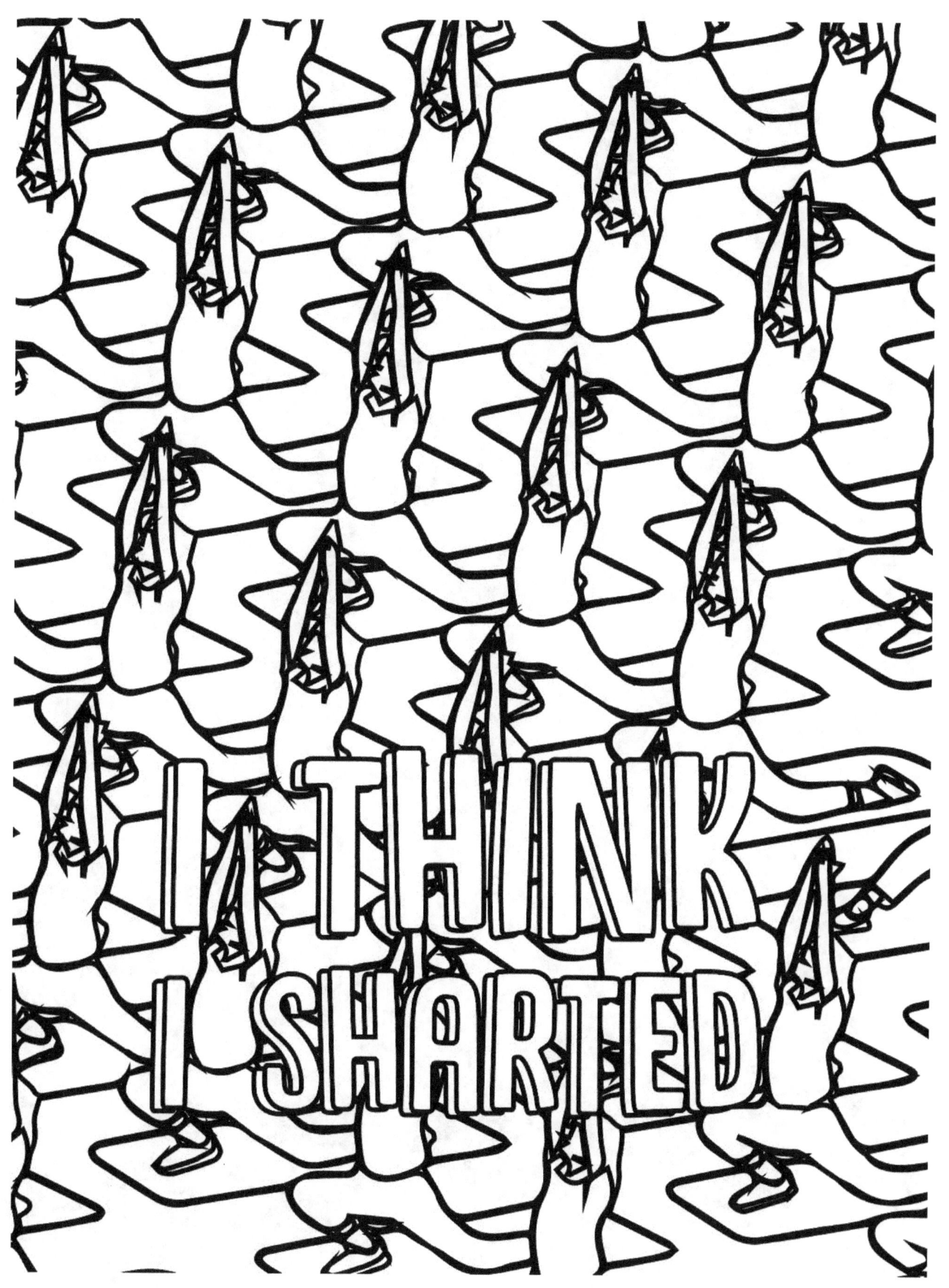

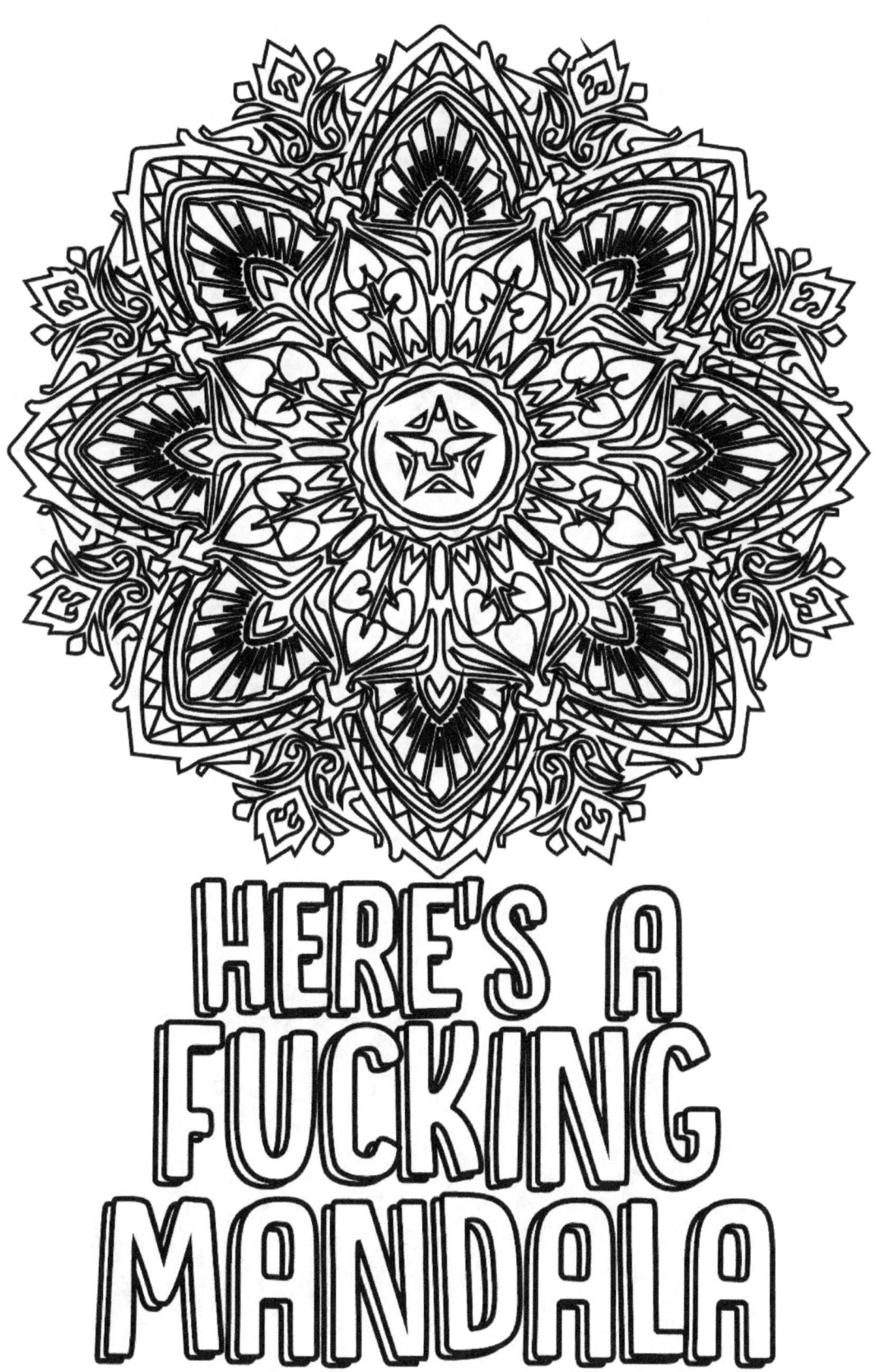

HERE'S A
FUCKING
MANDALA

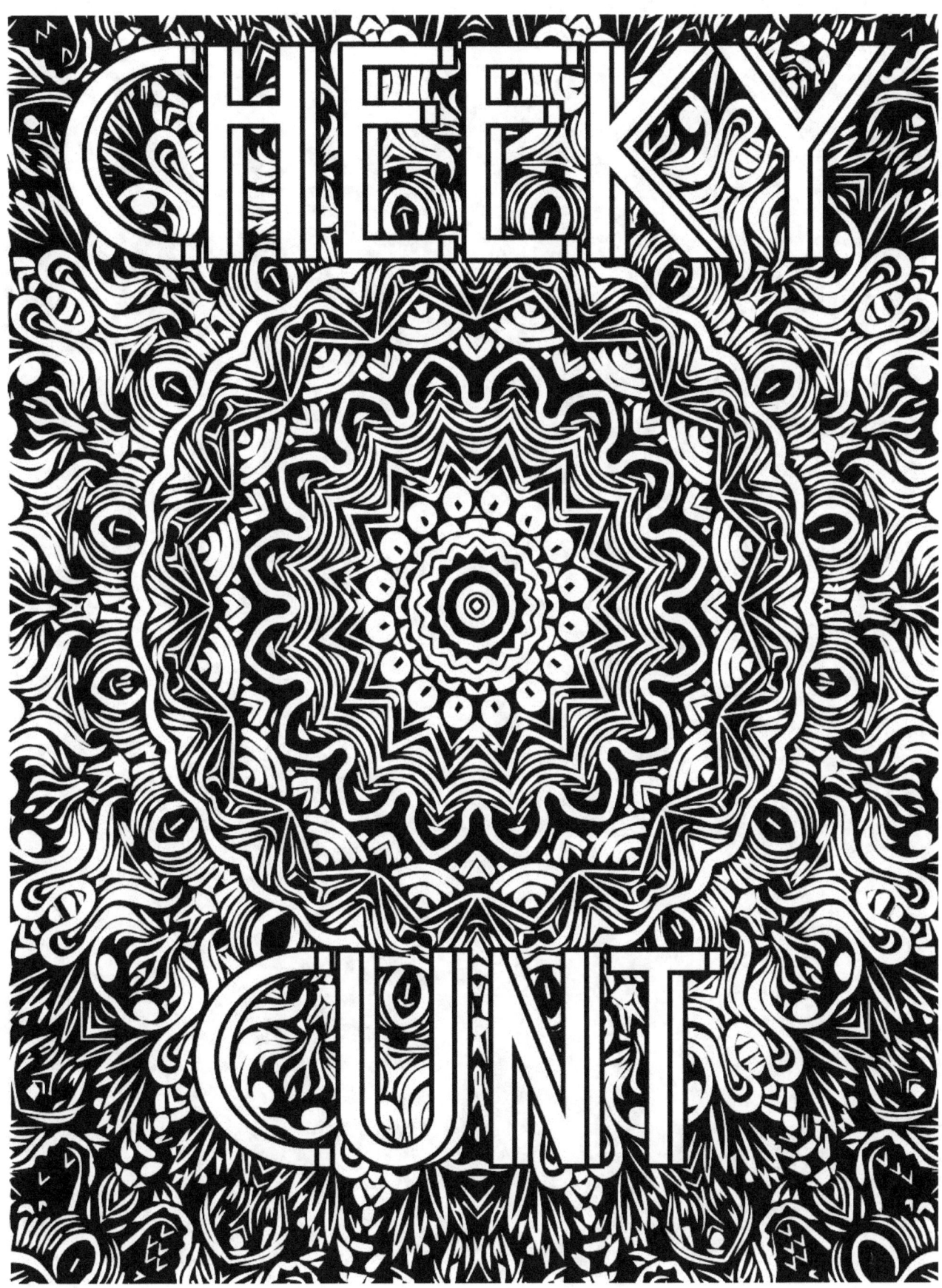

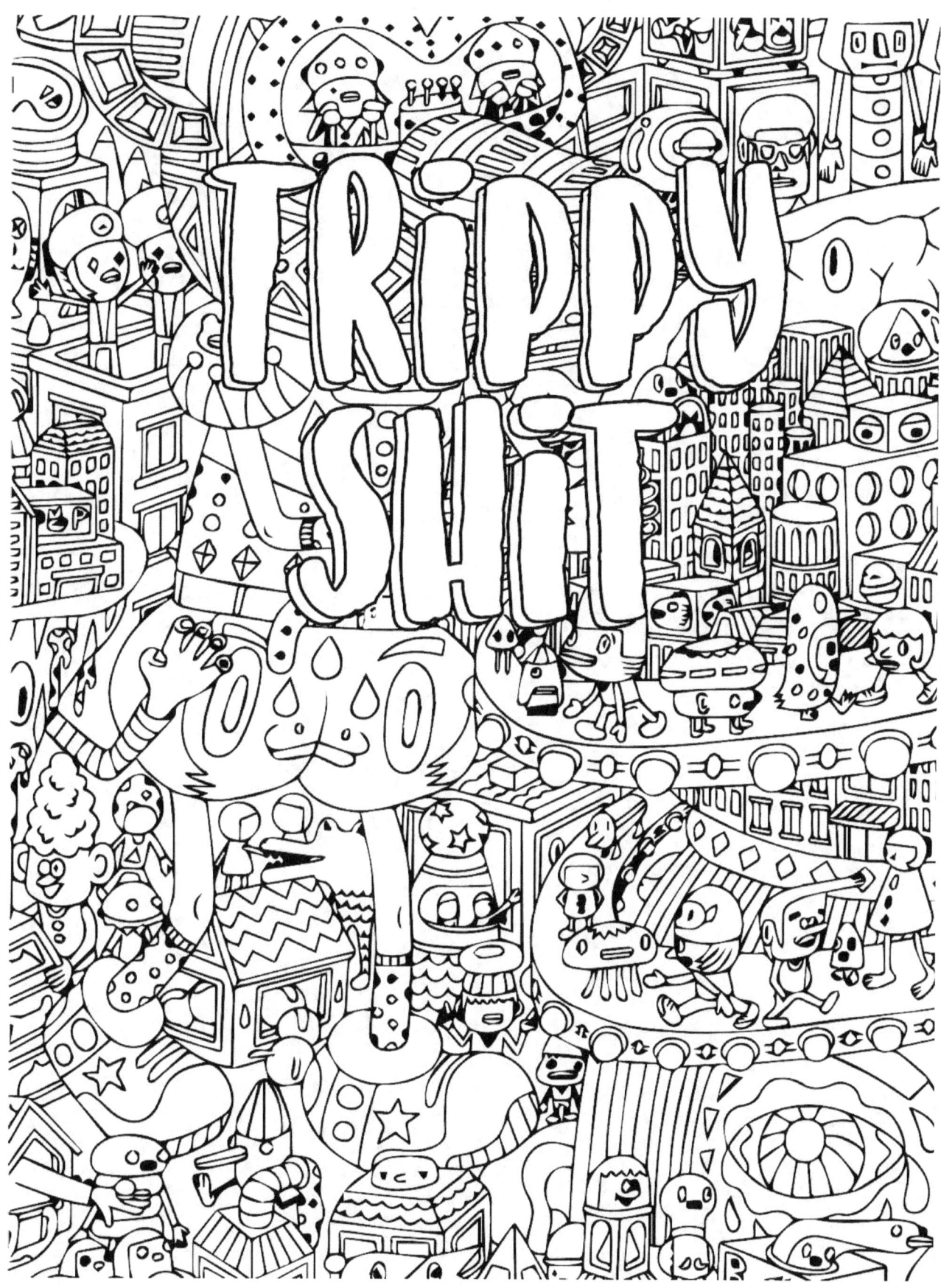

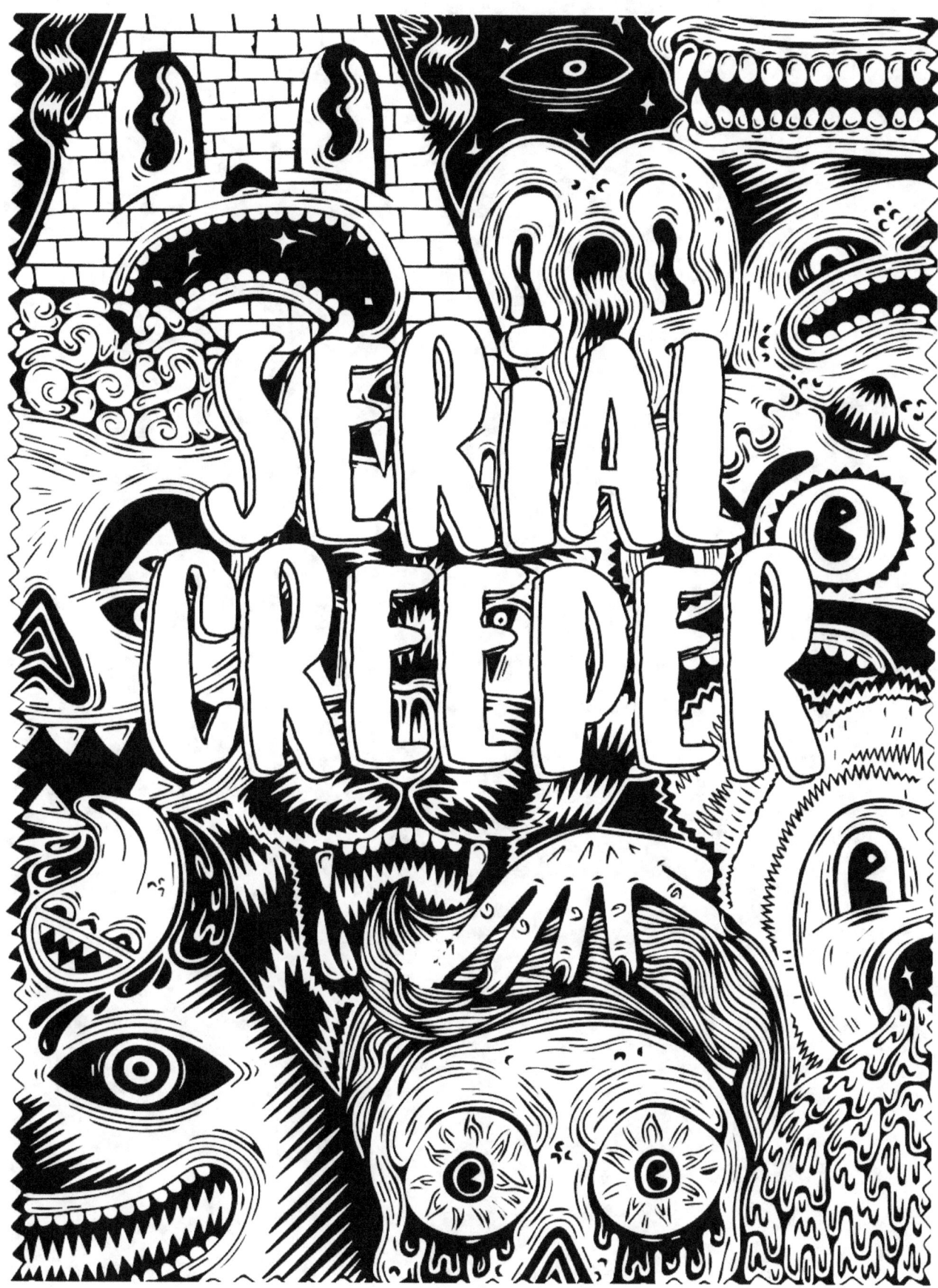

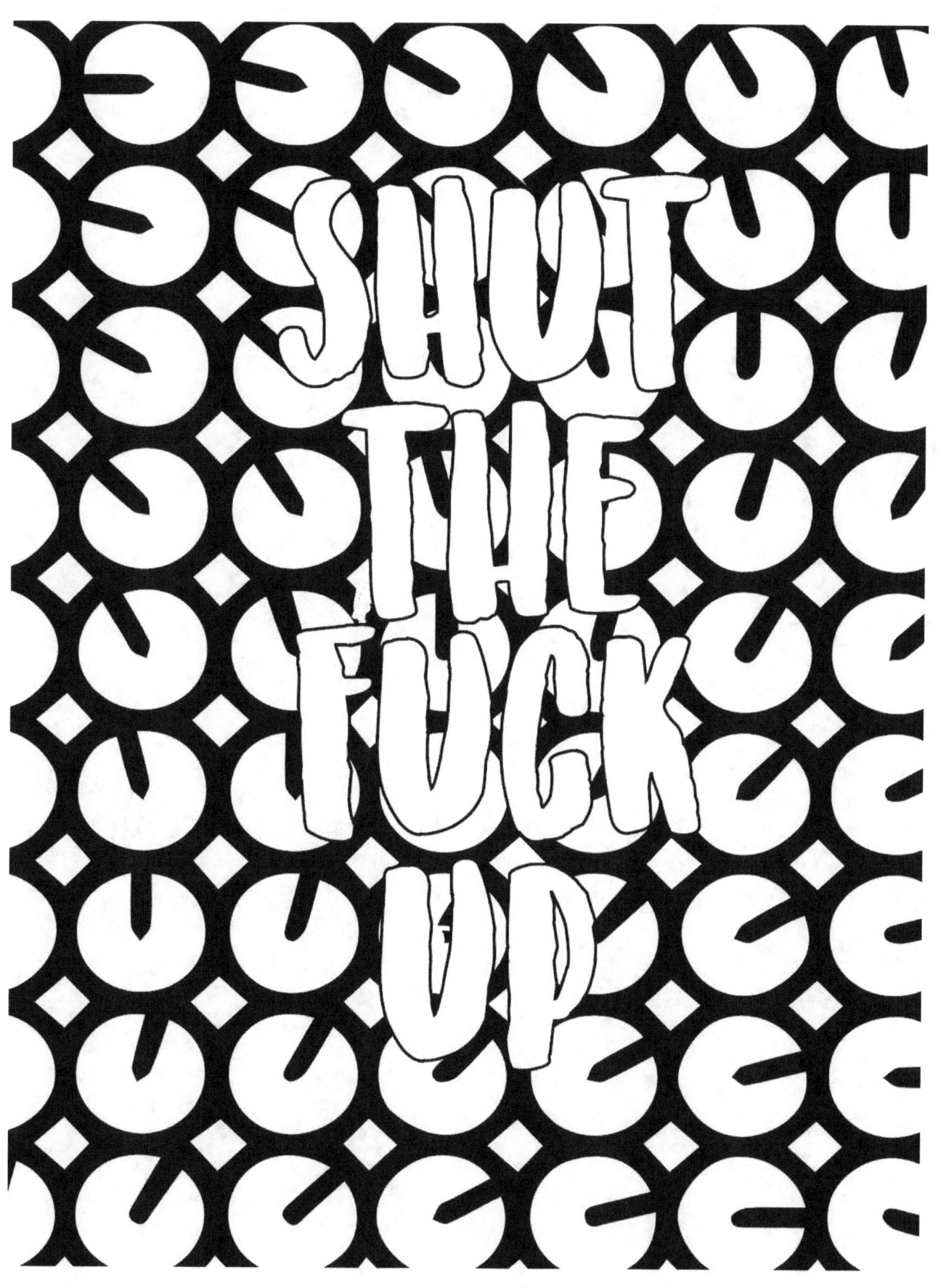

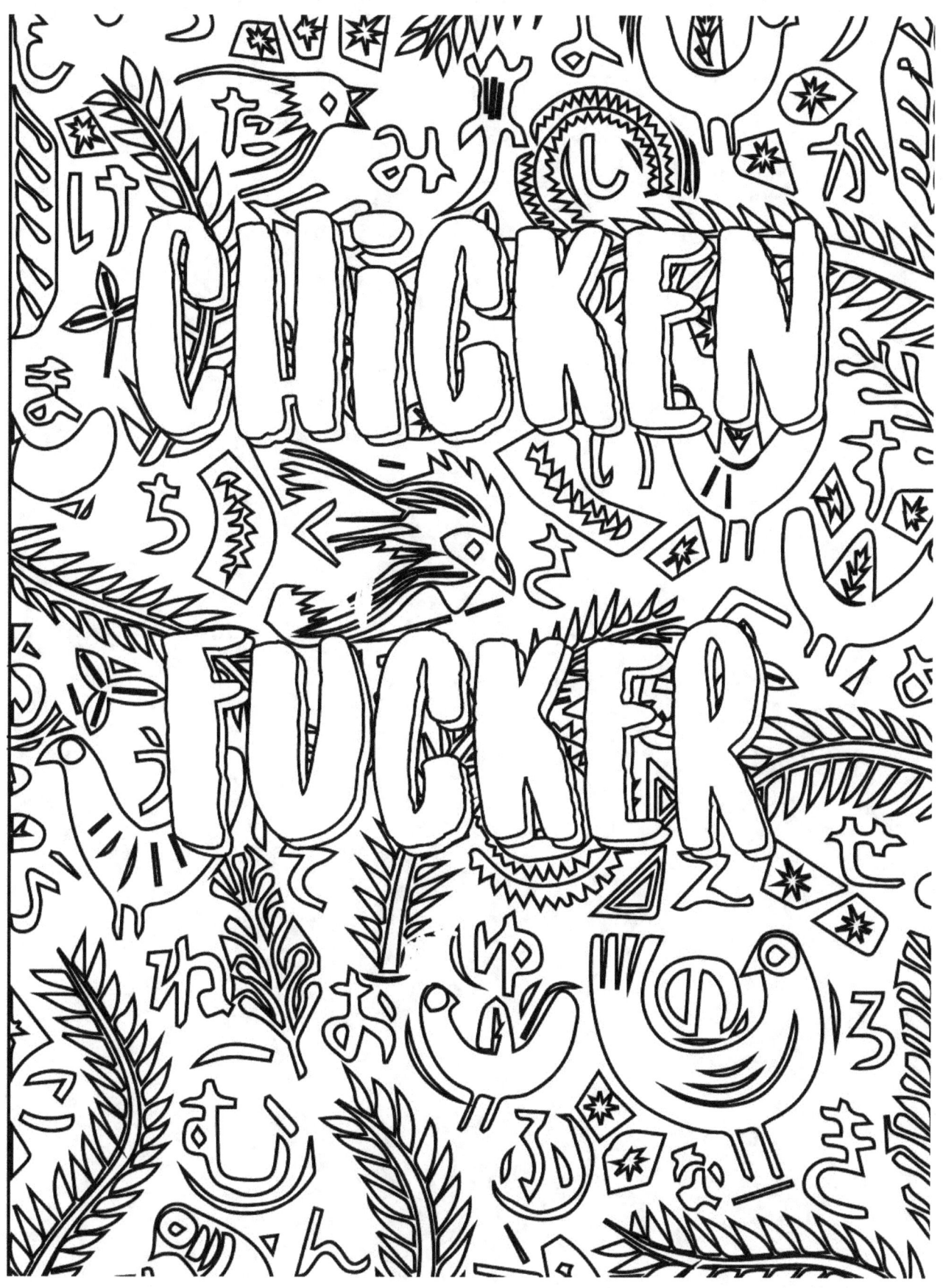

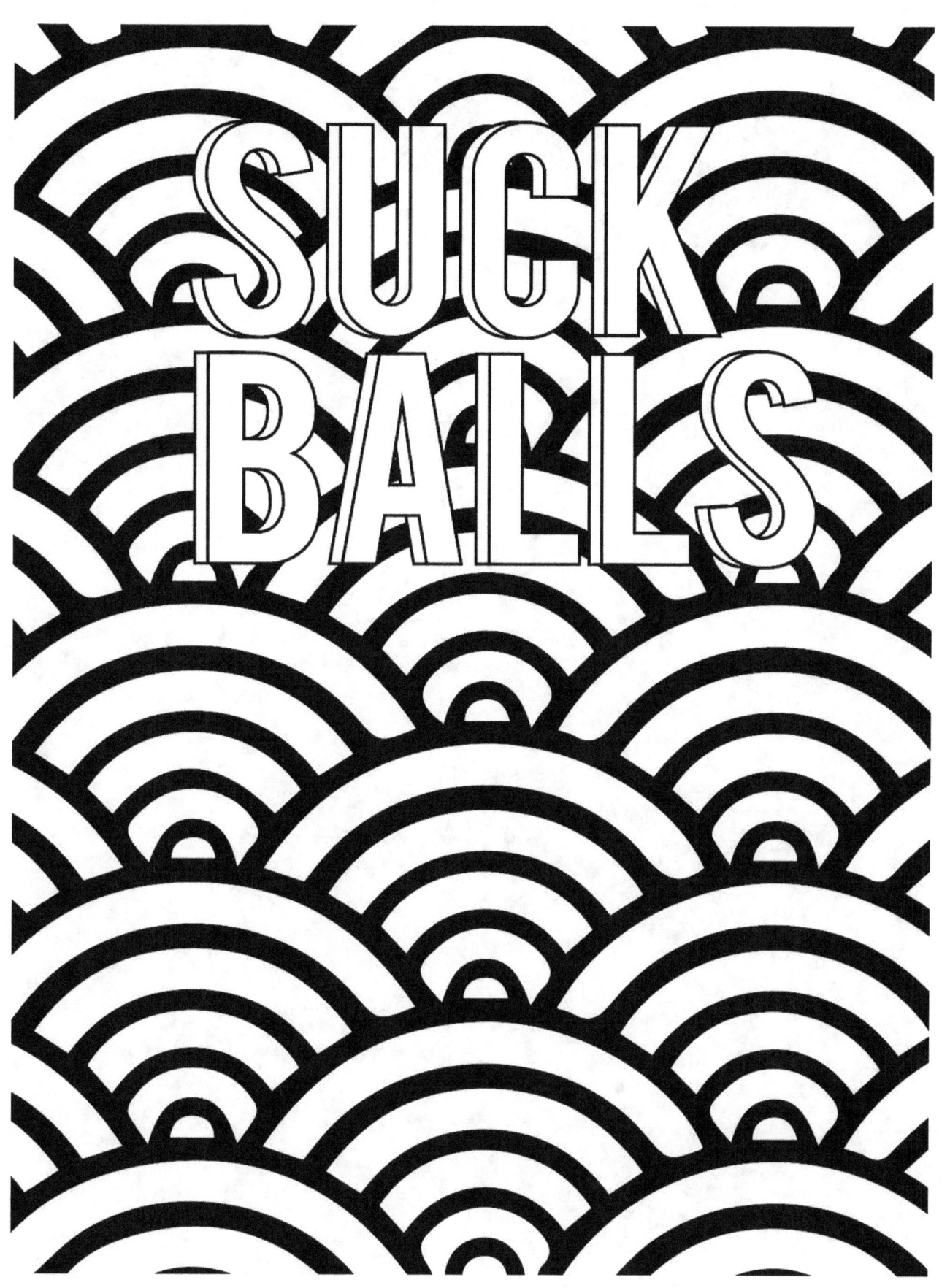

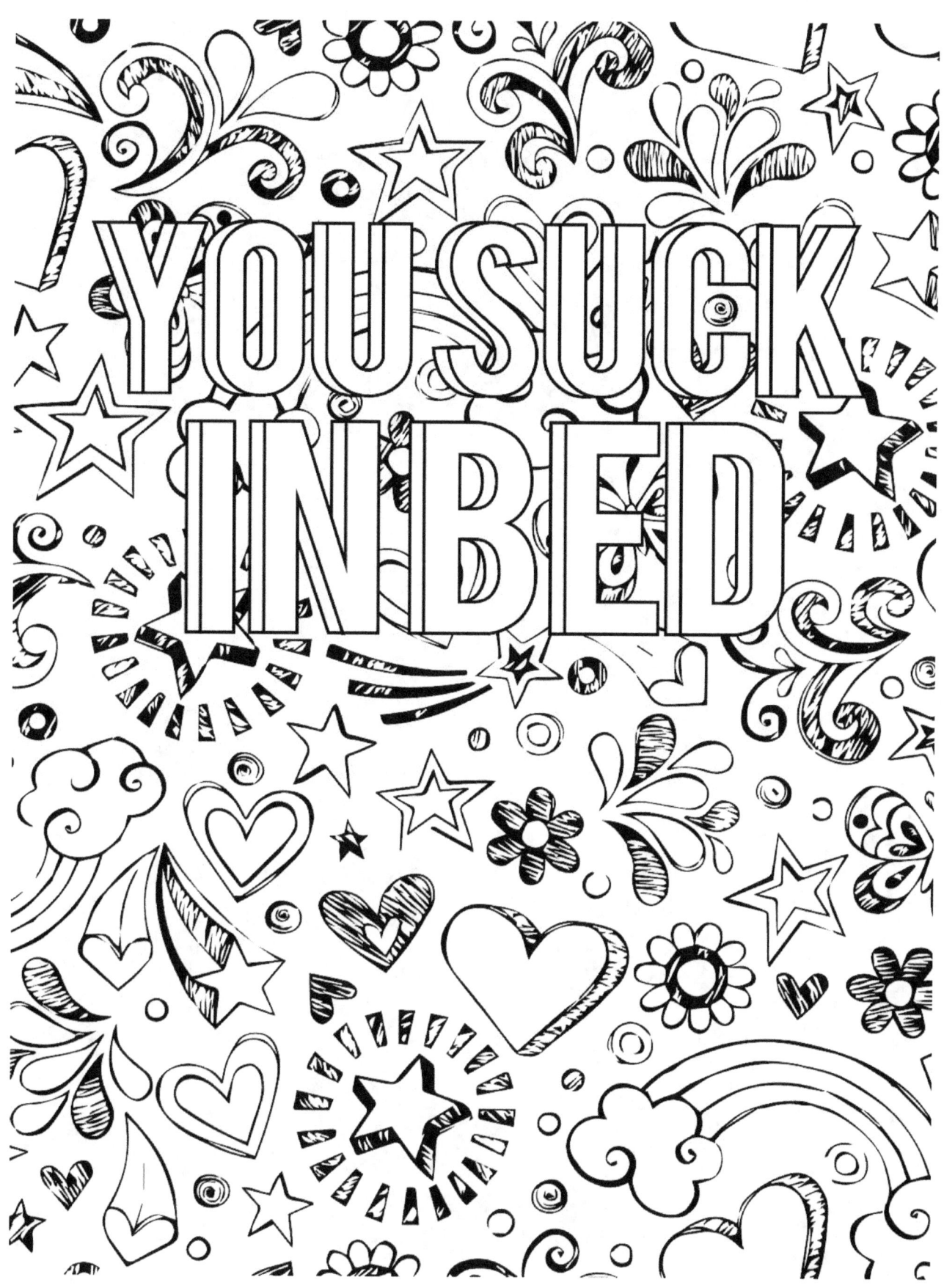

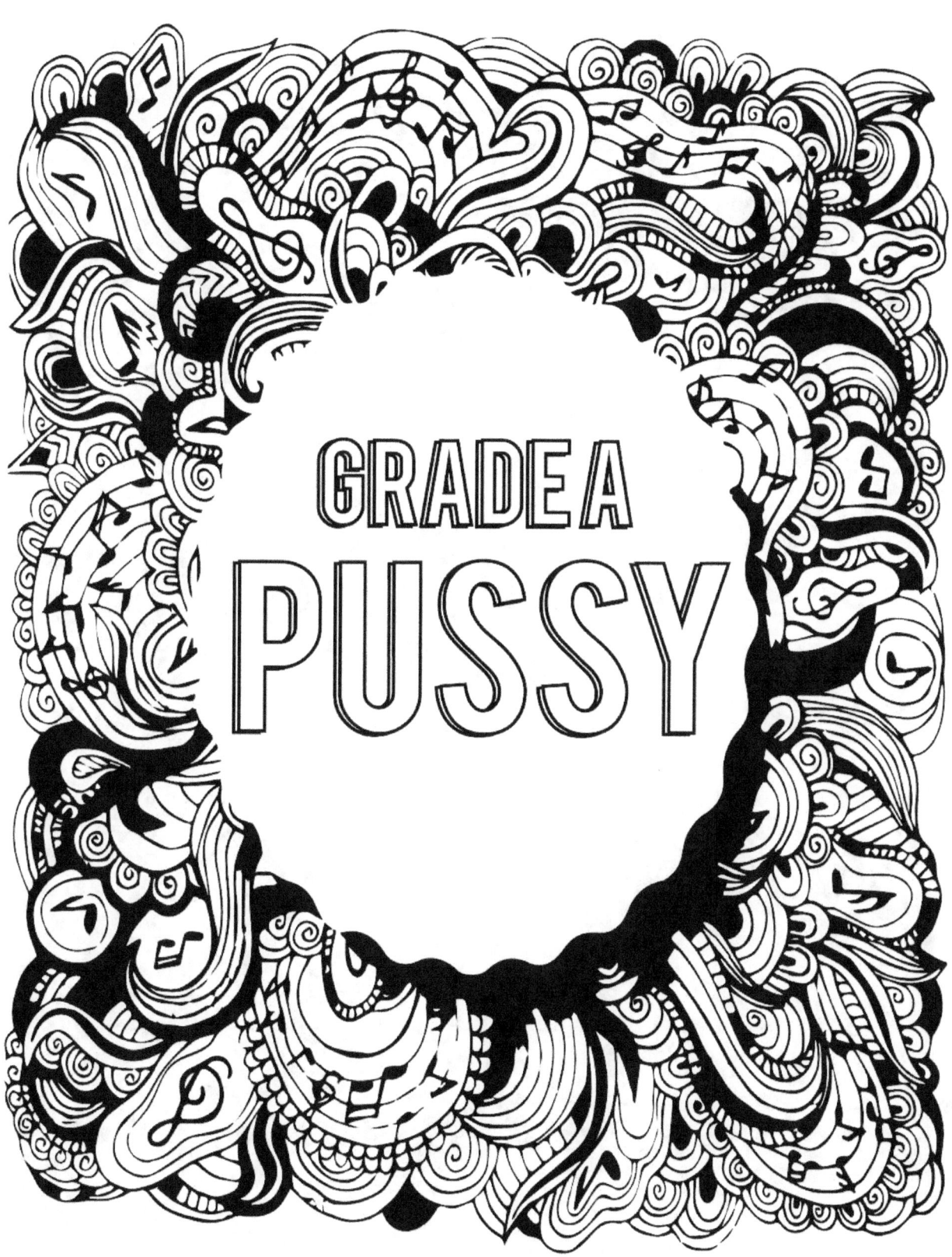

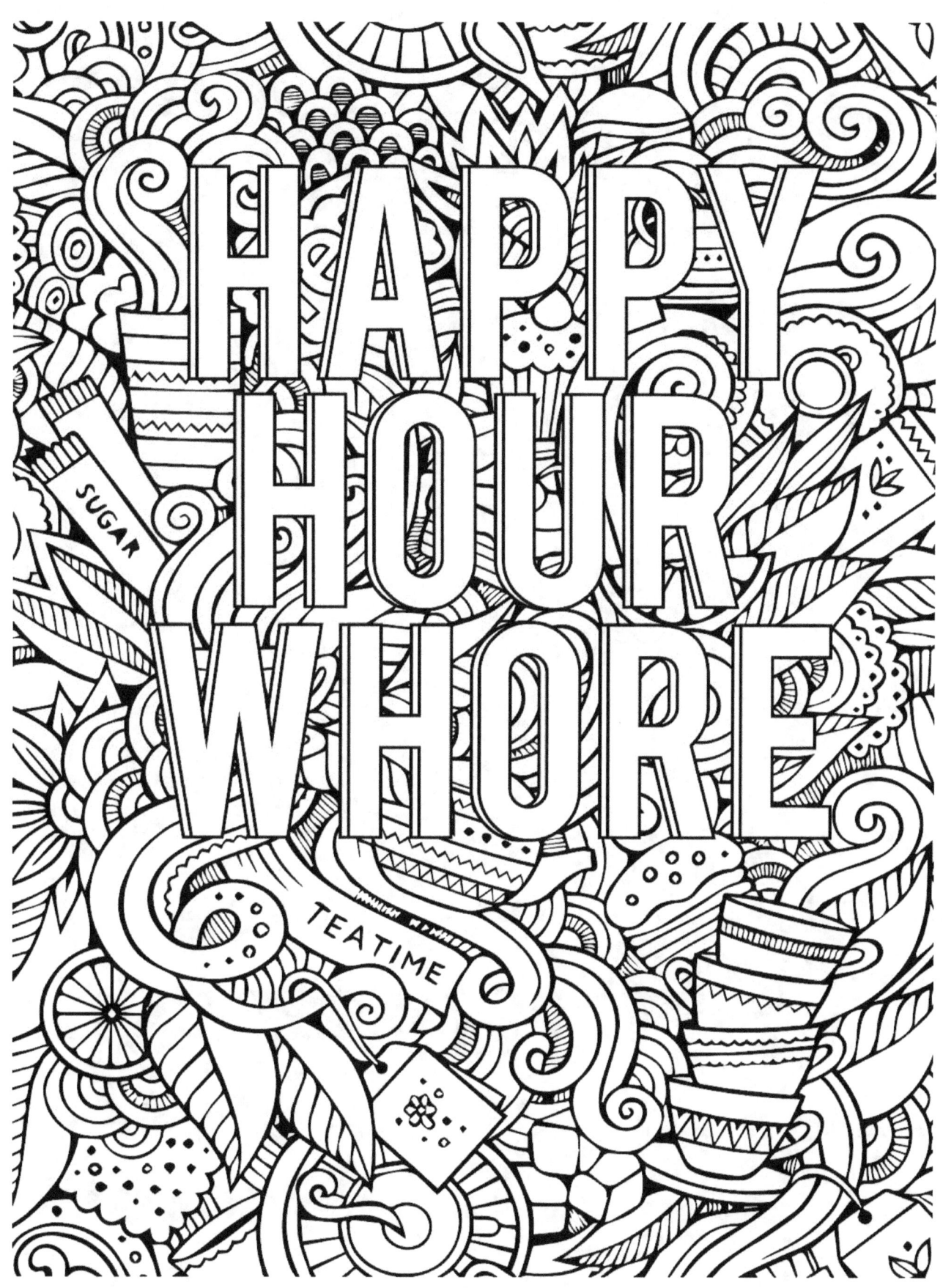

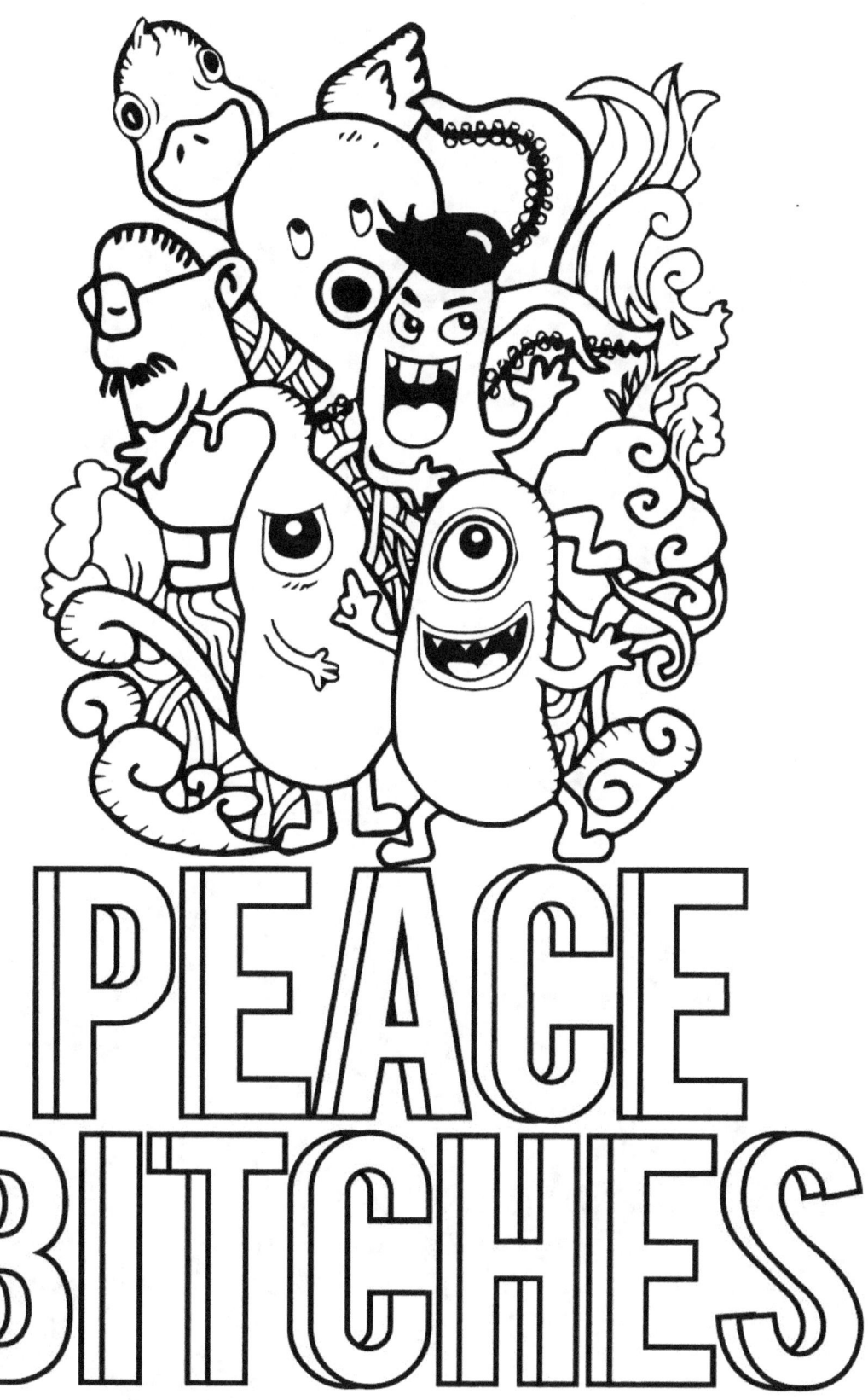

www.ingramcontent.com/pod-product-compliance
Lightning Source LLC
Chambersburg PA
CBHW081122180526
45170CB00008B/2964